First Guide to Government

What's a President and Vice President?

Nancy Harris

Heinemann Library
Chicago, Illinois

Customer Service 888-454-2279
Visit our website at **www.heinemannlibrary.com**

Designed by Kimberly R. Miracle and Betsy Wernert
Photo Research by Tracy Cummins
Maps provided by Map Specialists
Printed in China by South China Printing Company

11 10 09 08 07
10 9 8 7 6 5 4 3 2 1

ISBN-10: 1-4034-9465-7 (hc)   1-4034-9471-1 (pb)

Library of Congress Cataloging-in-Publication Data
Harris, Nancy, 1956-
   What's a president and vice president? / Nancy Harris.
      p. cm. -- (First guide to government)
   Includes bibliographical references and index.
   ISBN-13: 978-1-4034-9465-8 (hc) -- ISBN-13: 978-1-4034-9471-9 (pb)
   1. Presidents--United States--Juvenile literature. 2. Vice-Presidents--United States--Juvenile literature. 3. Separation of powers--
United States--Juvenile literature. I. Title.
   JK517.H37 2007
   352.230973--dc22

                             2007003262

Acknowledgments
The author and publishers are grateful to the following for permission to reproduce copyright material: Alamy **p. 6** (Glow Images);
AP Photo **pp. 13** (J. Scott Applewhite), 14 (Ken Heinen, Supreme Court), 22 (Kenneth Lambert); Jill Birschbach **p. 28**; David
Bohrerval White House Photo **p. 29**; Corbis **pp. 11** (Underwood & Underwood), 15 (Royalty Free), 17 (Michael Mulvey/Dallas
Morning News), 18 (FRED PROUSER/Reuters), 19 (MCNAMEE WALLY/SYGMA), 20 (Issei Kato/Reuters), 26 (Bettmann); Getty
Images **pp. 4** (Bruno Vincent), 5 (PAUL J. RICHARDS/AFP), 8 (Time & Life Pictures), 10 (Alex Wong), 12 (Ken Heinen), 16 (Time
& Life Pictures), 21 (Keystone), 23 (Mark Wilson), 24 (TOM MIHALEK/AFP), 25 (Time Life Pictures), 27 (Time Life Pictures).

Cover photograph reproduced with permission of Wally McNamee/CORBIS.

Every effort has been made to contact copyright holders of any material reproduced in this book. Any omissions will be rectified in
subsequent printings if notice is given to the publisher.

Disclaimer
All the Internet addresses (URLs) given in this book were valid at the time of going to press. However, due to the dynamic nature of
the Internet, some addresses may have changed, or sites may have changed or ceased to exist since publication. While the author
and publisher regret any inconvenience this may cause readers, no responsibility for any such changes can be accepted by either the
author or the publisher.

Contents

Who Is the President?.....................4
Head of State.........................5
The President and the Executive Branch 8
The President and the Legislative Branch.......10
The President and the Judicial Branch.........12
Commander in Chief 16
How Do You Become President? 18
Who Is the Vice President? 20
The Vice President and the Legislative Branch ...22
How Do You Become Vice President?.........24
How Long Can You Be President
     and Vice President? 26
Where They Live and Work.................28
Glossary............................30
More Books to Read....................31
Web Sites...........................31
Visiting the White House..................31
Index..............................32

Some words are shown in bold, **like this**. You can find out what they mean by looking in the glossary.

Who Is the President?

The president is the leader of the United States of America. The president makes decisions for the country. The president also represents the country to other nations.

president

★ The president of the United States meets with
★ leaders of other countries.

Head of State

One of the president's jobs is called **Head of State**. This means the president acts as a **symbol** of the United States to people around the world. This can include helping people in other countries.

The president represents what the United States believes in.

Capitol building

Supreme Court

★ The federal government is in Washington, D.C.

Many people work with the president to run the country. These people work for the **federal government**.

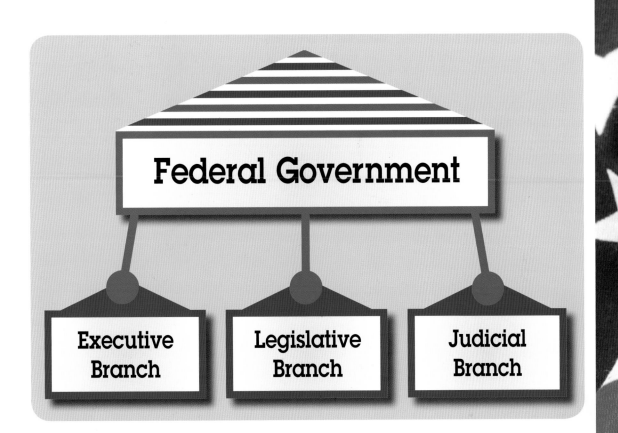

There are three branches (parts) of the federal government. Each branch has a different job. There are leaders in each branch.

The President and the Executive Branch

The president is the leader of the executive branch. The job of this branch is to make sure the **laws** in the country are followed. The president is the **chief executive** of this branch.

The president meets with members of the executive branch to make decisions about how to run the country.

The executive branch is divided into different departments (groups). The leader of each department is called the **secretary**. The **Cabinet** is made up of all the department secretaries. Cabinet members give the president advice.

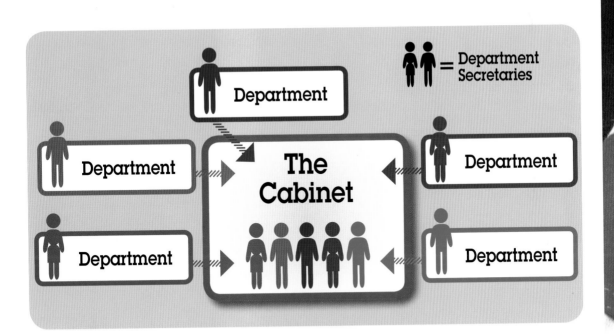

The President and the Legislative Branch

★★★ Members of the legislative branch hold meetings to discuss new bills.

The president works with the legislative branch. This branch makes **laws** for the United States. People who work in this branch propose (suggest) ideas for laws. The proposals are called **bills**.

★ President Kennedy is signing a bill.

People in the legislative branch vote to decide if a bill
should become a law. If they vote in favor of the bill,
it is sent to the president. If the president signs the bill,
it becomes a law.

The President and the Judicial Branch

The president works with the judicial branch. People who work in this branch make sure the **laws** are understood. They decide if a law has been broken.

★ Judges work in the judicial branch.

★★★ Sandra Day O'Connor served as a judge on the Supreme Court.

There are many **courts** in the judicial branch. A court is a place people can go if they feel a law has been broken. Judges work in courts.

★ Judges make decisions about laws.

Judges know the **law**. They make important decisions. They decide if laws are being followed correctly by the people and by the government.

★ The Supreme Court is in Washington, D.C.

The Supreme Court is the highest **court** in the judicial branch. The president chooses the judges for the Supreme Court. People in the legislative branch then vote to decide if they should become judges.

Commander in Chief

★ President Eisenhower is meeting with the armed forces.

The president is the **commander in chief**. This means the president is in charge of the **armed forces**. These are people who serve in the military. The president works with many others to lead the armed forces.

The armed forces protect our country. They include:

- The United States Army
- The United States Navy
- The United States Marines
- The United States Air Force
- The United States Coast Guard.

How Do You Become President?

The president is **elected** by the American people. People vote to choose who they want to lead the country. They choose from a list of people who are running for president.

★ People vote in private booths.

There are rules that say who can run for president. The rules are:

- You must be born in the United States.
- You must be at least 35 years old.
- You must have lived in the United States for at least 14 years.

★ Bill Clinton ran for president in 1992 and 1996. He won both times.

Who Is the Vice President?

The vice president is second in leadership under the president. The vice president acts as a **symbol** of the United States to people around the world. The vice president represents what the United States believes in.

★ The vice president meets with leaders of other countries.

★
★
★
Vice President Johnson became the president in 1963. This happened after President Kennedy was shot and killed.

The vice president supports the president. If the president can no longer serve, the vice president becomes president.

The Vice President and the Legislative Branch

The vice president is the president of the **Senate**. The Senate is part of the legislative branch. It helps make **laws** in the country. People in the Senate vote on a **bill** to decide if it should become a law.

★ The vice president meets with people in the Senate.

★ The vice president only votes in the Senate to break a tie vote.

Sometimes there is a tie vote. This means the same number of people vote for and against a bill. It is then up to the vice president to make the deciding vote.

How Do You Become Vice President?

★★★ George W. Bush chose Dick Cheney to run as his vice president.

The person running for vice president is chosen by the person running for president. The president and vice president run as a **pair**. They are **elected** by the American people.

There are rules that say who can run for vice president. The rules are:

- You must be born in the United States.
- You must be at least 35 years old.
- You must have lived in the United States for at least 14 years.

★★★★ People running for president and vice president must meet the same requirements.

How Long Can You Be President and Vice President?

★★★ President Reagan was elected for a second term as president.

A president is **elected** for a **term** of four years. After that, the president can run for president again. If the president is elected for a second term, he or she can serve for a total of eight years.

★ Al Gore served two terms as vice president.
★ He worked with President Bill Clinton.

Vice presidents can also serve a total of eight years. Sometimes vice presidents run for president. They can then serve eight more years as president.

Where They Live and Work

The president lives and works in the White House. The vice president lives in a house called the Admiral's House. The vice president works in the White House and in the **Senate**. Both houses are in Washington, D.C.

★ This is the White House.

The president and vice president have very important jobs. They help lead the country. They represent the United States to people around the world.

★ This is the Admiral's House.

Glossary

armed forces people who serve in the military. The armed forces include the Army, Air Force, Coast Guard, Navy, and Marines.

bill written idea for a new law (rule)

Cabinet group of department secretaries who give advice to the president

chief executive leader of the executive branch. This branch of government makes sure the laws (rules) in the country are being followed.

commander in chief person in charge of the armed forces. The president of the United States is commander in chief.

court place where people meet to decide if a law has been understood

elect choose a person to serve in a leadership position

federal government group of leaders who run the entire country. In a federal government, the country is made up of many states.

Head of State person who represents the United States to people around the world

law rule people must obey in a state or country

pair two people who do something together

secretary leader of a department (group) in the executive branch

Senate group of people who work in Congress. They are called senators. They help make the laws (rules) in the United States.

symbol object or thing that stands for something else. For example, the American flag stands for the United States and its values.

term length of time that a person serves in a leadership position

More Books to Read

An older reader can help you with these books:
Dubois, Muriel. *The U.S. Presidency*. Mankato, MN: Capstone Press, 2004.

January, Brendan. *The Presidency*. New York: Scholastic, 2005.

Web Sites

Ben's Guide to Government gives young readers information about how the United States government works. http://bensguide.gpo.gov/

The White House for Kids Web site has biographies of past presidents and vice presidents. It also has information about our current leaders. http://www.whitehouse.gov/kids/

Visiting the White House

You can visit the White House Tuesday through Saturday from 7:30 am to 12:30 pm.

The White House address is:
The White House
1600 Pennsylvania Avenue NW
Washington, D.C. 20500

Index

Admiral's House 28-29

armed forces 16-17

bill 10-11, 22-23

court 13, 15

Cabinet 9

chief executive 8

commander in chief 16

executive branch 7, 8-9

Head of State 5

judge 12-15

judicial branch 7, 12-13, 15

legislative branch 7, 10-11, 15, 22

Senate 22-23, 28

Supreme Court 13, 15

White House 28